NO LONGER PROPERTY OF
ANYTHINK LIBRARIES/
RANGEVIEW LIBRARY DISTRICT

anythink

VEGETABLES!

Life on a Produce Farm

by Ruth Owen

WINDMILL
BOOKS

New York

Published in 2012 by Windmill Books, an Imprint of Rosen Publishing
29 East 21st Street, New York, NY 10010

Copyright © 2012 Ruby Tuesday Books Ltd

Adaptations to North American edition © 2012 Windmill Books, An Imprint of Rosen Publishing

All rights reserved. No part of this book may be reproduced in any form without permission in writing from the publisher, except by a reviewer.

Editor for Ruby Tuesday Books Ltd: Mark J. Sachner
U.S. Editor: Julia Quinlan
Designer: Emma Randall
Consultant: Logan Peterman, Laughing Sprout Family Farm

Photo Credits: Cover, 1, 4–5, 6–7, 8–9, 10–11, 12–13, 14–15, 16–17, 18–19, 20–21, 22–23, 24–25, 26–27, 28–29, 30–31 © Shutterstock.

Library of Congress Cataloging-in-Publication Data

Owen, Ruth, 1967–
Vegetables! : life on a produce farm / by Ruth Owen.
p. cm. — (Food from farmers)
Includes index.
ISBN 978-1-61533-531-2 (library binding) — ISBN 978-1-61533-540-4 (pbk.) —
ISBN 978-1-61533-541-1 (6-pack)
1. Vegetables—Juvenile literature. 2. Farm produce—Juvenile literature. 3. Farm life—Juvenile literature. I. Title. II. Title: Life on a produce farm. III. Series: Food from farmers.
SB324.O94 2012
635—dc23

2011026649

Manufactured in the United States of America

CPSIA Compliance Information: Batch #BOW2102WM: For Further Information contact Windmill Books, New York, New York at 1-866-478-0556

CONTENTS

WELCOME TO MY FARM!

Hi! My name is Jenny. I am 11 years old. I live on a **produce** farm with my mom and dad. We grow around 40 different types of vegetables on our farm.

Our farm is an **organic** farm.
This means we don't use any chemicals.

Mom

Dad

4

Most farms use **chemicals** to feed their plants. They also use chemicals to kill **pests** such as vegetable-munching insects.

An organic farmer watches how nature does things. Then the farmer uses those natural ways to grow crops. We grow vegetables in a way that is kind to planet Earth.

My favorite vegetables are carrots.

Charlie's Cool Vegetable Facts

• Nature made carrots purple or yellow, not orange! Vegetable growers in the Netherlands figured out how to grow orange carrots about 350 years ago.

LET'S LOOK AROUND THE FARM

This is a map of our farm. We live in the farmhouse.

Corn

Peas

Horse paddock

Lake

Potatoes

Cabbages

Carrots

Beets

Salad crops

Onions

Beehives

Peppers

Broccoli

Lettuces

Squash and pumpkins

Greenhouses

Chickens

Shed

Farmhouse

Our land is divided into lots of small fields.

This is a field of pea plants.

Each of these baby plants will grow into a cabbage.

The peas are inside the pods.

Pod

Clare helps on the farm in spring.

This is one of our greenhouses.

Some of our vegetable plants start their lives in the greenhouses.
Some vegetables, such as tomatoes, grow better in a warm greenhouse.

Charlie's Cool Vegetable Facts

- **There are thousands of different types of tomatoes grown around the world!**

We keep horses, chickens, and bees on the farm, too.
I will tell you more about the important jobs they do later in the book.

WHAT DO WE GROW?

Small produce farms often grow lots of different vegetable crops.

Sometimes one of our crops will die or not grow well. This can happen if the weather gets too hot. It can also happen if the weather is too cold or there is too much rain. Different crops grow best in different types of weather. So growing lots of different crops makes good sense.

Some of our crops grow underground.

Onions

Beets

Potatoes

Carrots

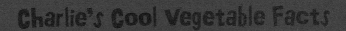

Charlie's Cool Vegetable Facts

- When people chop onions, it often makes their eyes water. This is because the onions are releasing a gas. It's the same kind of gas that comes out of a volcano when it erupts!

Some of our crops grow above ground.

Lettuce   Eggplants   Chili peppers   Corn

Cucumbers   Broccoli

IT ALL BEGINS WITH THE SOIL!

Vegetable plants grow best in soil that is filled with **nutrients**. Nutrients are all the good things a plant needs to help it grow.

Tiny living things called microorganisms live in soil.

You can't see the microorganisms without a microscope!

Soil microorganisms do an important job. They help dead plants, dead animal bodies, and animal **manure** break down, or rot. Plants get the nutrients they need from

Organic farmers fill their soil with rotted natural material.

Rotting tree bark and leaves

Many farms that are not organic use chemicals to feed their plants.
These chemicals can kill the microorganisms in the soil.
They can also make insects, birds, and other wild animals sick.
The chemicals may stay in the vegetables or fruit that people eat!

MAKING MUCK!

We make natural food to feed our vegetables.
The food is made from old plants and manure.
We call it organic muck!

Any leftover crops from last year are allowed to rot.

We collect manure from our horses and chickens.

Manure and straw from the animal barns

The muck does more than just feed the plants.
It also makes the soil lumpier and stronger.
This means water stays in the soil and doesn't soak away
so fast. A plant that has water and plenty of nutrients will
be healthy and strong.

Charlie's Cool Plant Facts

• **Strong, healthy plants are better at fighting off diseases.
This means organic farmers don't have to use chemicals
to kill plant diseases.**

In late winter, the tractor
plows up the soil in the fields.

Then we spray muck onto
the soil.

Now the fields are ready for
planting in spring.

PLANTING TIME

During the winter, Dad buys the seeds for next year's crops. We buy seeds from an organic seed company. I help Dad order the seeds online.

It's easy to see what some seeds will grow into.

Pea seeds

Other seeds are harder to guess.

Beet seeds

Some seeds are planted in soil called **compost**. These seeds grow in trays inside the greenhouse.

In late spring it is warm enough for the little plants to be planted outside.

Lettuce seeds

Some seeds are planted in rows in the fields.

Charlie's Cool Farm Facts

• Insect pests learn to come to a field where there is a crop they like. Organic farmers plant different vegetables in each field each year. Moving crops around makes it harder for the pests to find them!

THE TOMATO CROP

Every year we plant thousands of tomato seeds.

There are a lot of seeds inside a tomato!

In the greenhouse, the seeds grow into tomato plants.

The plants grow yellow flowers. Inside each flower is a yellow dust called **pollen**. The pollen must be moved from the male part of the flower to the female part. This is called **pollination**. Once a flower is pollinated, it can produce seeds. Our bees do this important job.

We put a beehive in the greenhouse.
The bees visit the flowers.
Pollen sticks to their furry bodies and gets moved around inside the flowers.
Now the flowers can produce seeds.

Beehive

16

Charlie's Cool Bee Facts

- Bees visit the tomato flowers to collect a sweet liquid called **nectar**, which they eat.
- A bee can pollinate up to 30 flowers in a minute!

The flowers give their seeds a fleshy, protective covering—tomatoes!

Tiny tomato

The tomatoes grow bigger and turn from green to red. Now they are just right for picking!

THE POTATO CROP

Every year, we grow thousands of potatoes on our farm!

These potatoes are known as seed potatoes. Each one of the shoots will grow into a potato.

Shoot

The seed potatoes are planted in rows in the field.

A plant grows from each seed potato. The potato plants get bigger.

Under each plant, lots of potatoes are growing.

Looks at what's happening underground!

Plant stem

Potato

Roots

When the plants start to go yellow and die, the potatoes are ready. Dad puts a potato plow on the back of the tractor. The plow is like a giant shovel. It digs into the ground and lifts up the potatoes.

The potatoes are collected in boxes and sacks.

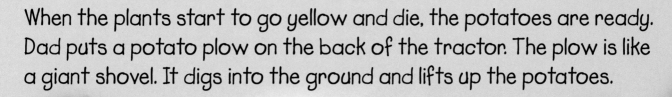

Charlie's Cool Vegetable Facts

• Including French fries, an adult American eats about 140 pounds (63.5 kg) of potatoes every year!

PROTECTING OUR CROPS

Lots of insect pests want to eat the crops that farmers grow.

Pests can be killed by chemicals called **pesticides**. The problem is that the pesticides may kill every insect around. They may also harm other wild animals.

Ladybug eating aphids

Aphids

Aphids are tiny insects that kill plants by sucking the juices out of them. Organic farmers have a natural way of getting rid of pests such as aphids. We get insects, such as ladybugs, to eat the aphids.

Ladybugs also eat pollen and nectar from flowers.
We plant flowers around our fields.

The ladybugs come to the flowers to eat pollen and nectar.
Then they eat the aphids in the field that attack our
vegetable plants!

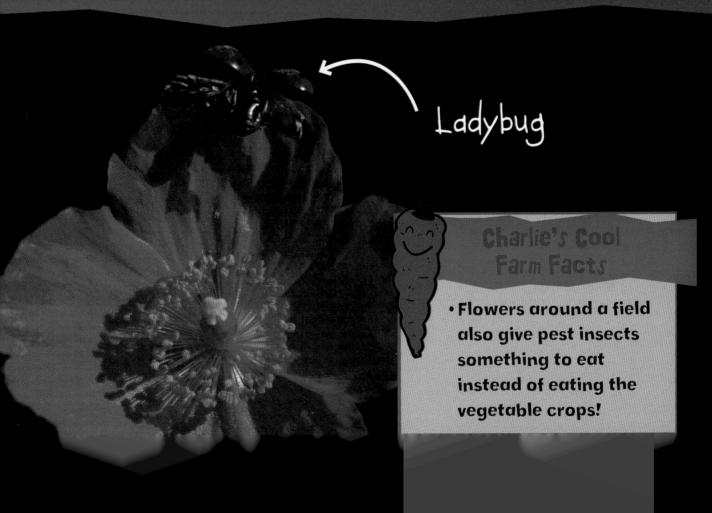

Ladybug

Charlie's Cool Farm Facts

- Flowers around a field also give pest insects something to eat instead of eating the vegetable crops!

HARVEST TIME

In the summer and fall there are crops
to be harvested every week!

Mom and Dad can't do all the work on the farm.
Often students who are studying farming at college
come here to help out for a few weeks.

Tom is harvesting zucchini.
He uses a knife to cut the
zucchini off the plant.

Mark works on the farm
every summer.
Mark is picking corn.

I like to help Dad harvest the carrots.

These onions have been pulled out of the soil. We dry them in the sun before putting them into sacks.

Every day. Dad delivers boxes of our produce to local food stores.

Charlie's Cool Vegetable Facts

- A tomato is really a fruit because it has seeds inside. In 1893, however, the U.S. Supreme Court ruled that tomatoes should be called vegetables.

VEGETABLES FOR SALE!

We sell our vegetables to local supermarkets, small stores, and restaurants.

We also sell vegetable boxes to people in nearby towns.
A vegetable box contains enough vegetables for a family for a week.

We choose all the freshest things that have just been harvested.
Dad delivers the boxes in the truck.

On Saturdays we have a stand at a farmers' market.

At the market, local farmers sell the things they grow and make. You can buy fruit, wine and cider, meat, bread, and cheese.

I help Mom take care of the stand.

Charlie's Cool Vegetable Facts

- We all want to save energy. Buying locally-grown produce cuts down on the amount of fuel used. The food may only travel a few miles from the farm to the store or market.

27

A DAY IN THE LIFE OF A FARM

Farming families work very hard!

7:00 a.m.
Dad checks the plants in the greenhouses. He waters the plants and looks for insect pests!

Insect pest

9:00 a.m.
Mom and Dad pack vegetable boxes for our customers. The boxes include potatoes, onions, carrots, tomatoes, and lots of other freshly-picked vegetables.

11:00 a.m.
Mom is pulling **weeds** in the fields.

Charlie's Cool Vegetable Facts

• Weeds can block the Sun's light and use up lots of water. This can make crops weak and sick.

Parsley

Weed

1:00 p.m.
Dad delivers the vegetable boxes.

3:00 p.m.
Dad plows up a field of clover. We planted the clover to feed the soil.
The clover will now rot and add lots of nutrients to the soil.

4:00 p.m.
Dad digs up lettuces, while
Mom picks tomatoes.

7:00 p.m.
Grandma and Grandpa
come for supper.
They also collect
their weekly supply
of vegetables!

27

WE LOVE VEGETABLES!

Vegetables give us so many great tastes to choose from! They are also very good for our bodies.

Vegetables contain **fiber** that keeps your **digestive system** working well. A baked potato has more fiber than a bowl of bran cereal!

Eating vegetables makes your heart and eyes healthier. The **vitamin** A in carrots helps you see in the dark!

The substance in tomatoes that makes them red helps protect your body against cancer.

Grandma teaches me how to cook!

Everyone should eat at least two servings of fruit and three servings of vegetables every day. I like to cook these vegetable dishes.

Homemade vegetable pizza

Chicken and vegetable kebabs

Stir fry vegetables and noodles

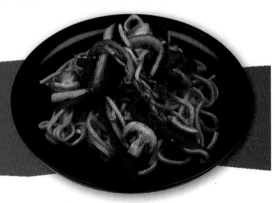

Thank you to vegetable farmers everywhere!

Charlie's Cool Vegetable Facts

• Try to eat as many different colored vegetables as possible. The more colorful the vegetable, the better it is for you.

GLOSSARY

chemicals (KEH-mih-kulz)
Matter that can be mixed with other matter to cause changes.

compost (KOM-pohst)
Crumbly soil filled with nutrients that is used by farmers and gardeners for planting seeds and young plants.

crops (KROPS)
Plants that are grown in large quantities on a farm.

digestive system (dy-JES-tiv SIS-tem)
The group of body parts, such as the stomach, that break down food so that a body can use it for fuel.

fiber (FY-ber)
Material found in plants. Your body can't break down fiber, so it pushes it through your digestive system, which helps keep your poop moving out of your body.

manure (muh-NOOR)
Animal waste.

nectar (NEK-tur)
A sweet liquid made by flowers.

nutrients (NOO-tree-ents)
Substances that a living thing needs to help it live and grow. Foods contain nutrients such as vitamins.

organic farm (or-GA-nik FARM)
A farm that doesn't use chemicals to feed crops or kill insect pests and weeds. Organic farms are kinder to planet Earth.

pest (PEST)
An animal or plant that damages or kills crops.

pesticides (PES-tuh-sydz)
Substances, usually made from chemicals, that kill pests.

pollen (PAH-lin)
A yellow dust produced by the male part of a flower called the anther.

pollination (pah-luh-NAY-shun)
Moving pollen from the male part of a flower to the female part so that a plant can reproduce (make more plants) by making seeds.

produce (PROH-doos)
Fresh fruit or vegetables.

vitamin (VY-tuh-min)
A substance found in foods that is needed by the body for health and growth.

weed (WEED)
A plant growing where it is not wanted. Weeds are often tough, wild plants that grow very quickly.

WEB SITES
For Web resources related to the subject of this book, go to: www.windmillbooks.com/weblinks and select this book's title.

READ MORE

Edwards, Nicola. *Vegetables. See How Plants Grow.* New York: PowerKids Press, 2007.

Gibbons, Gail. *The Vegetables We Eat.* New York: Holiday House, 2008.

McCorquodale, Elizabeth. *Kids in the Garden: Growing Plants for Food and Fun.* London, UK: Black Dog Publishing, 2010.

INDEX